AUSTRALIAN WILD

AN AUSTRALIAN ANIMAL COLOURING BOOK

ISABEL JEPPE

Boyd's forest dragon | *Hypsilurus boydii*

Boyd's forest dragon | *Hypsilurus boydii*

budgerigar | *Melopsittacus undulatus*

budgerigar | *Melopsittacus undulatus*

butterfly gurnard | *Lepidotrigla vanessa*

butterfly gurnard | *Lepidotrigla vanessa*

Cairns birdwing butterfly | *Ornithoptera euphorion*

Cairns birdwing butterfly | *Ornithoptera euphorion*

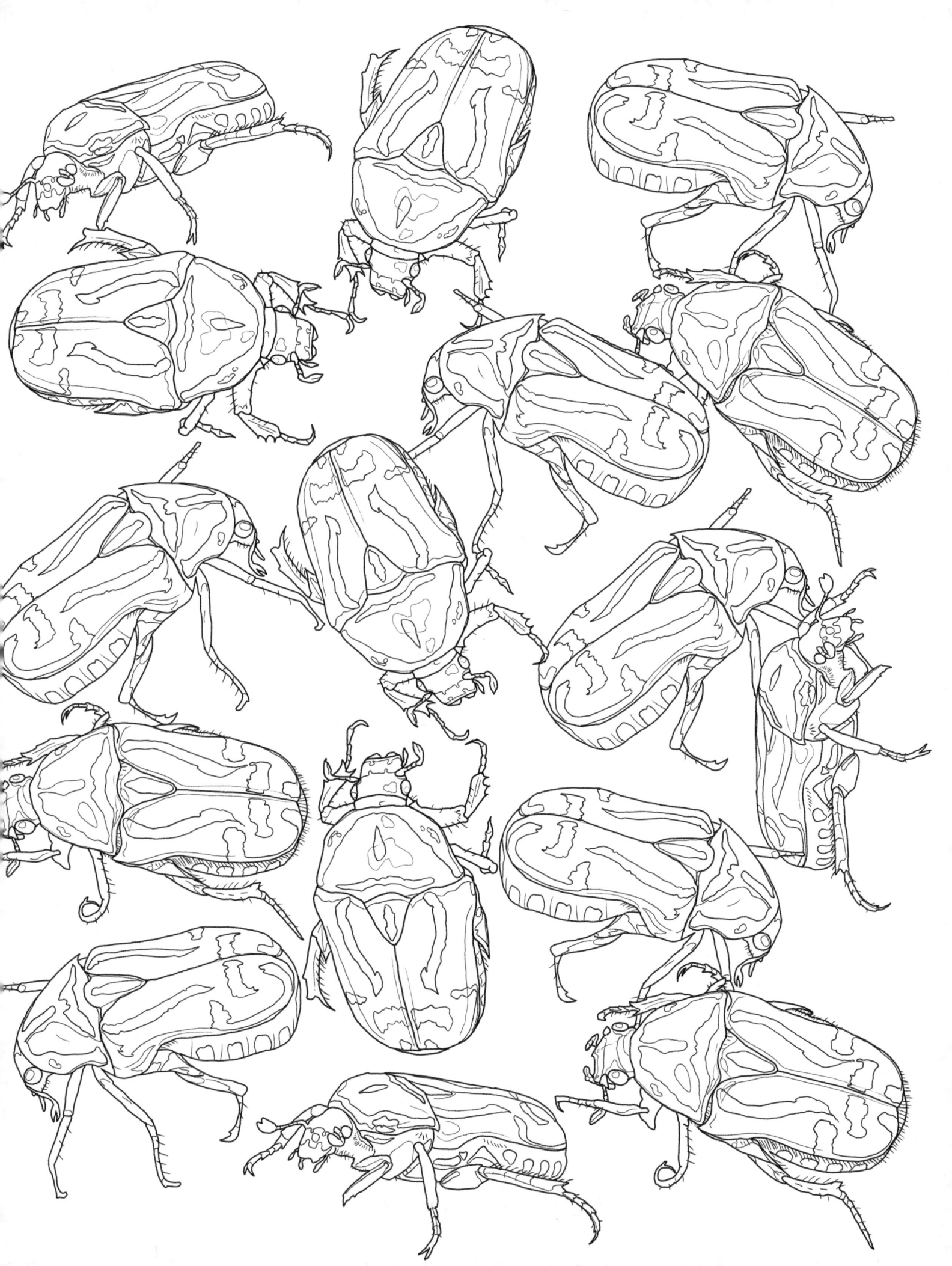

fiddler beetle | *Eupoecila australasiae*

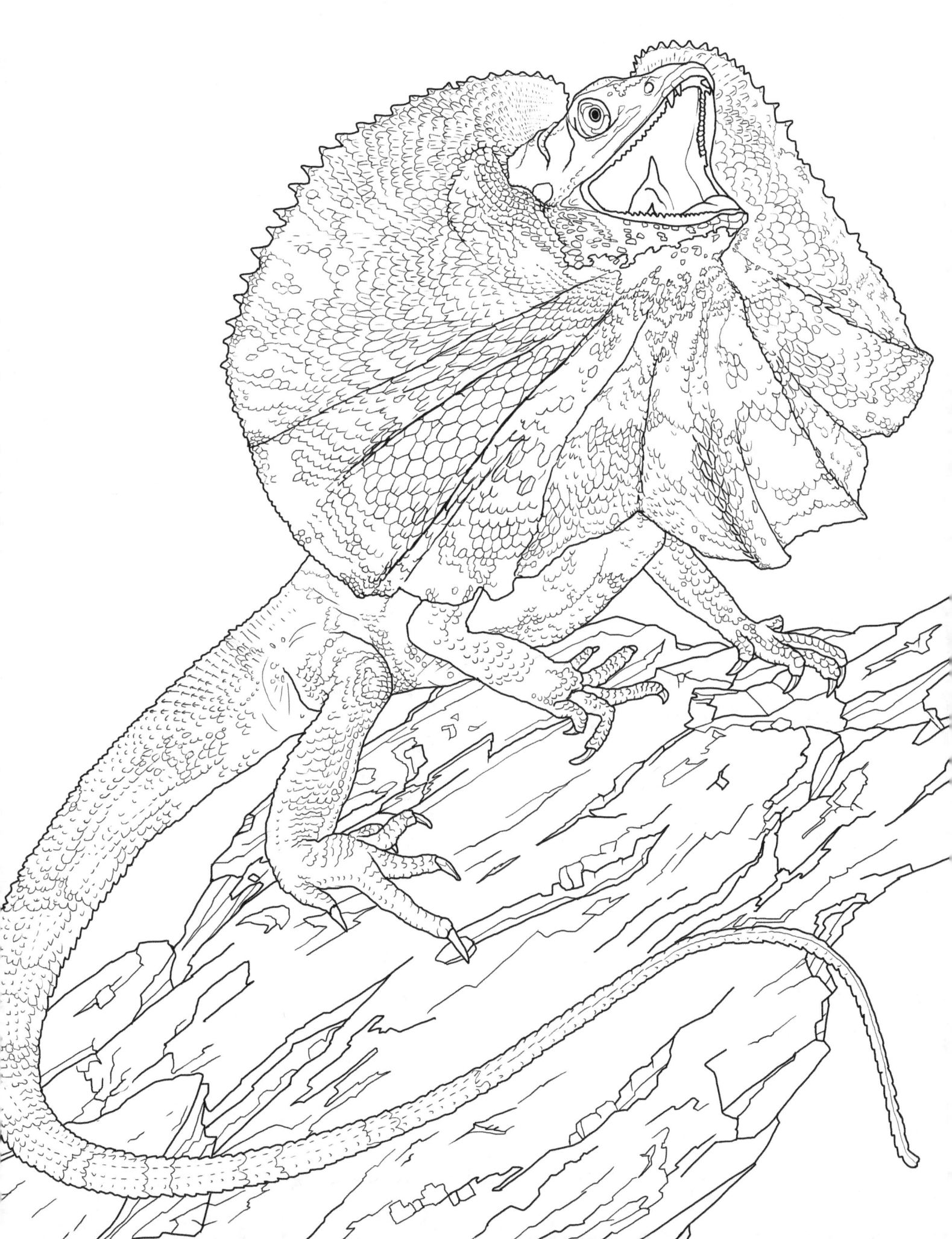

frilled-neck lizard | *Chlamydosaurus kingii*

frilled-neck lizard | *Chlamydosaurus kingii*

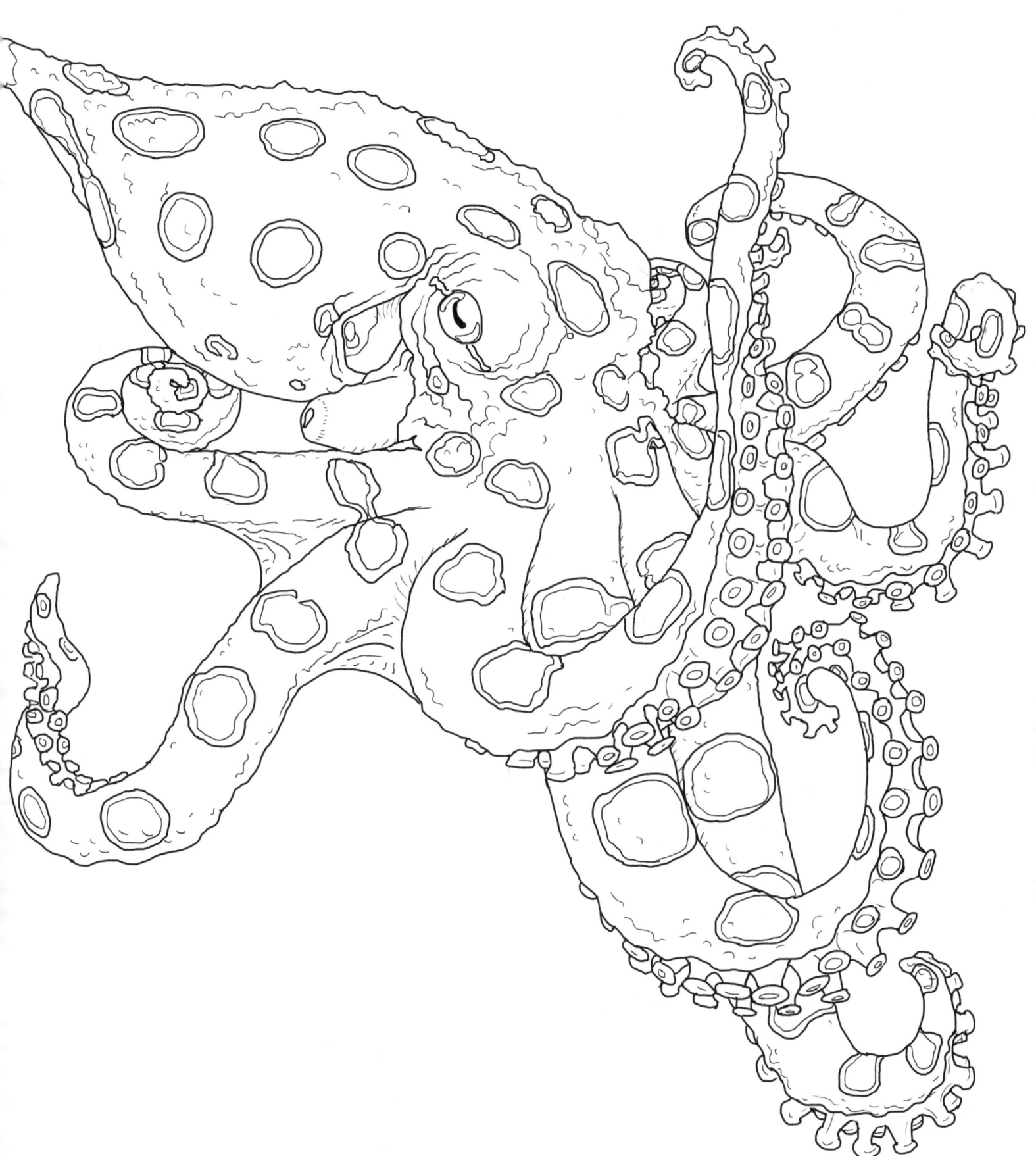

greater blue-ringed octopus │ *Hapalochlaena lunulata*

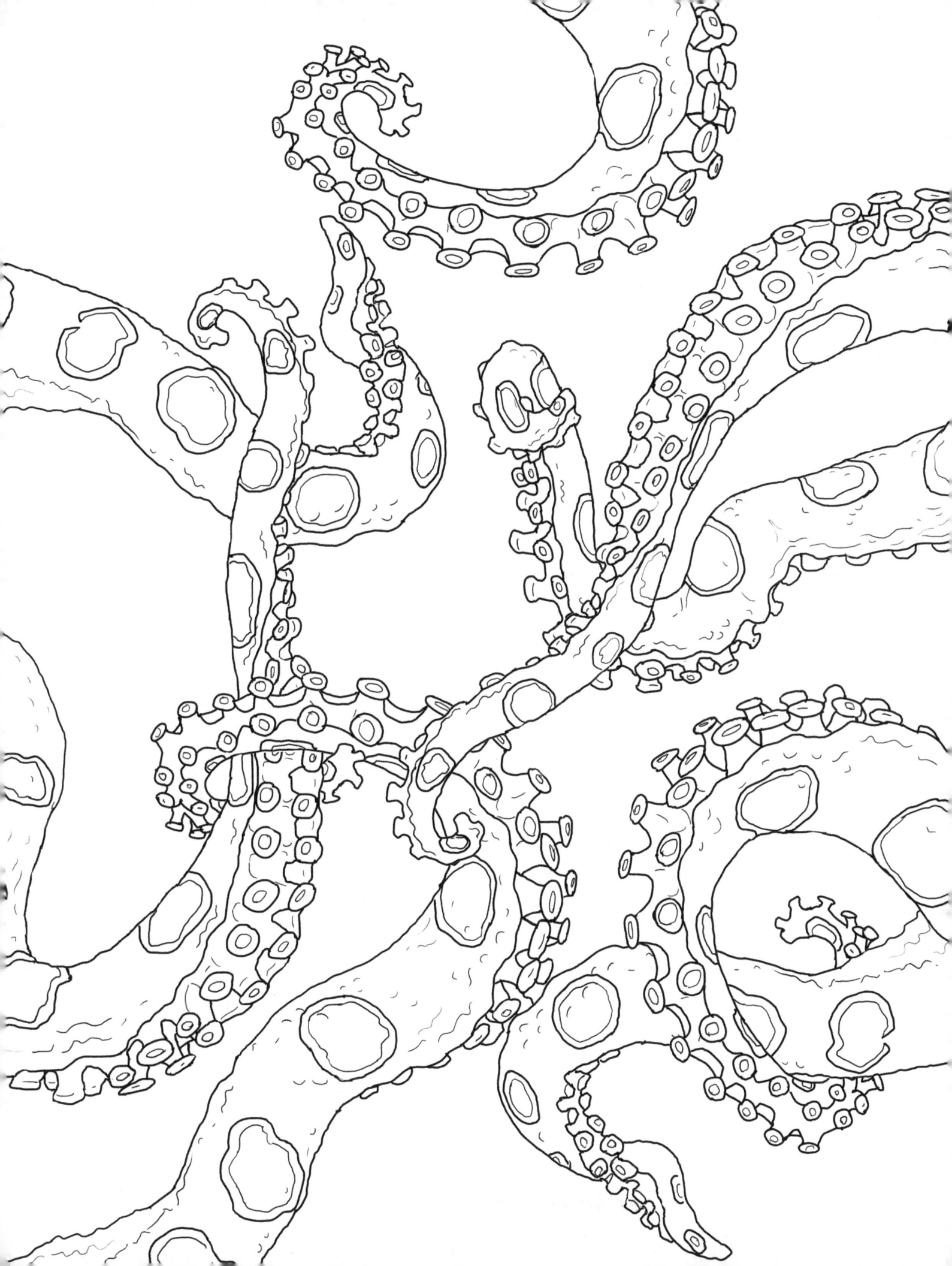

greater blue-ringed octopus | *Hapalochlaena lunulata*

leafy seadragon | *Phycodurus eques*

leafy seadragon | *Phycodurus eques*

Leichhardt's grasshopper | *Petasida ephippigera*

Leichhardt's grasshopper | *Petasida ephippigera*

numbat | *Myrmecobius fasciatus*

numbat │ *Myrmecobius fasciatus*

Peacock spider | *Maratus volans*

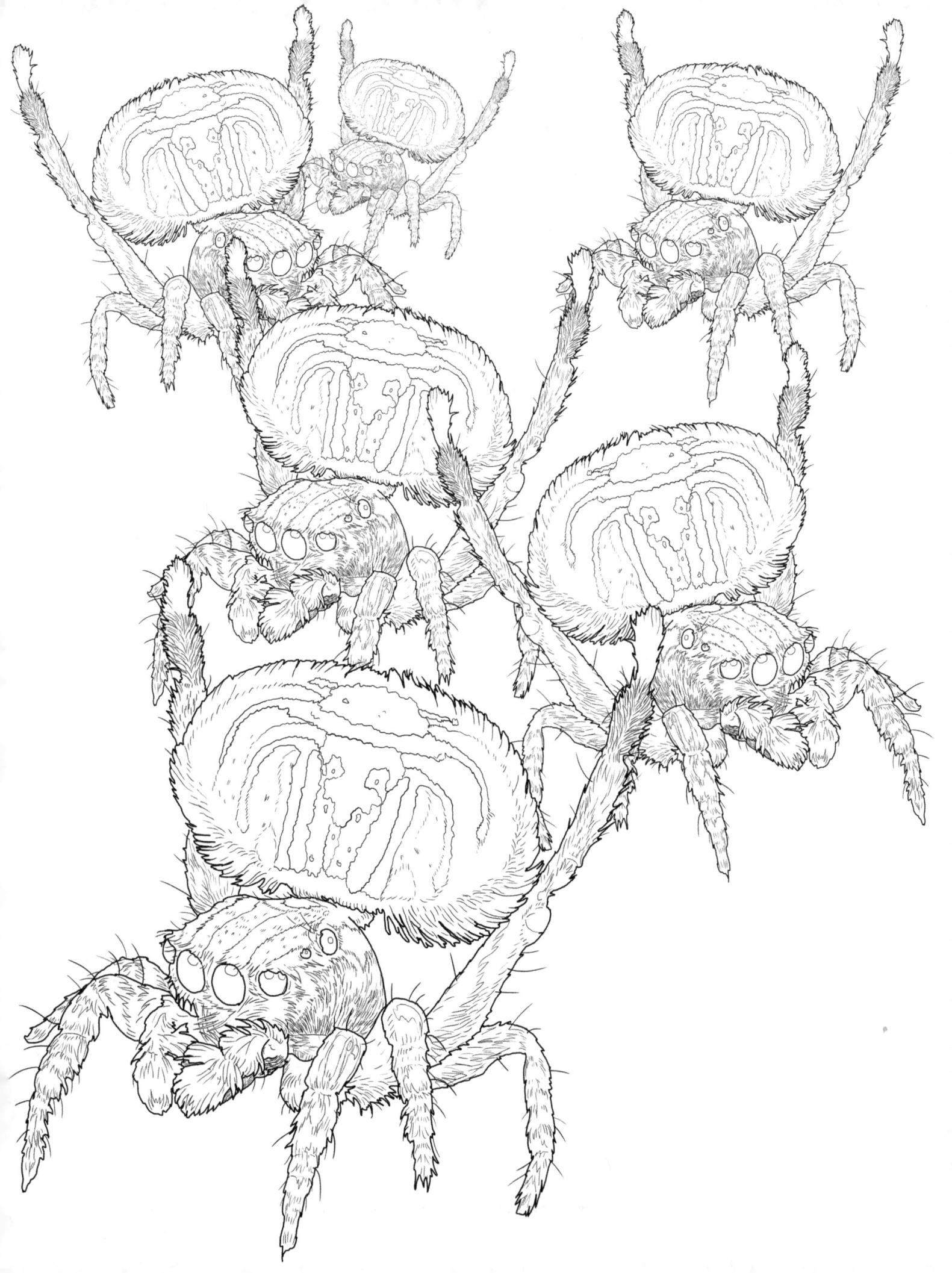

Peacock spider | *Maratus volans*

quokka | *Setonix brachyurus*

quokka | *Setonix brachyurus*

rainbow lorikeet | *Trichoglossus moluccanus*

rainbow lorikeet | *Trichoglossus moluccanus*

short-beaked echidna | *Tachyglossus aculeatus*

short-beaked echidna | *Tachyglossus aculeatus*

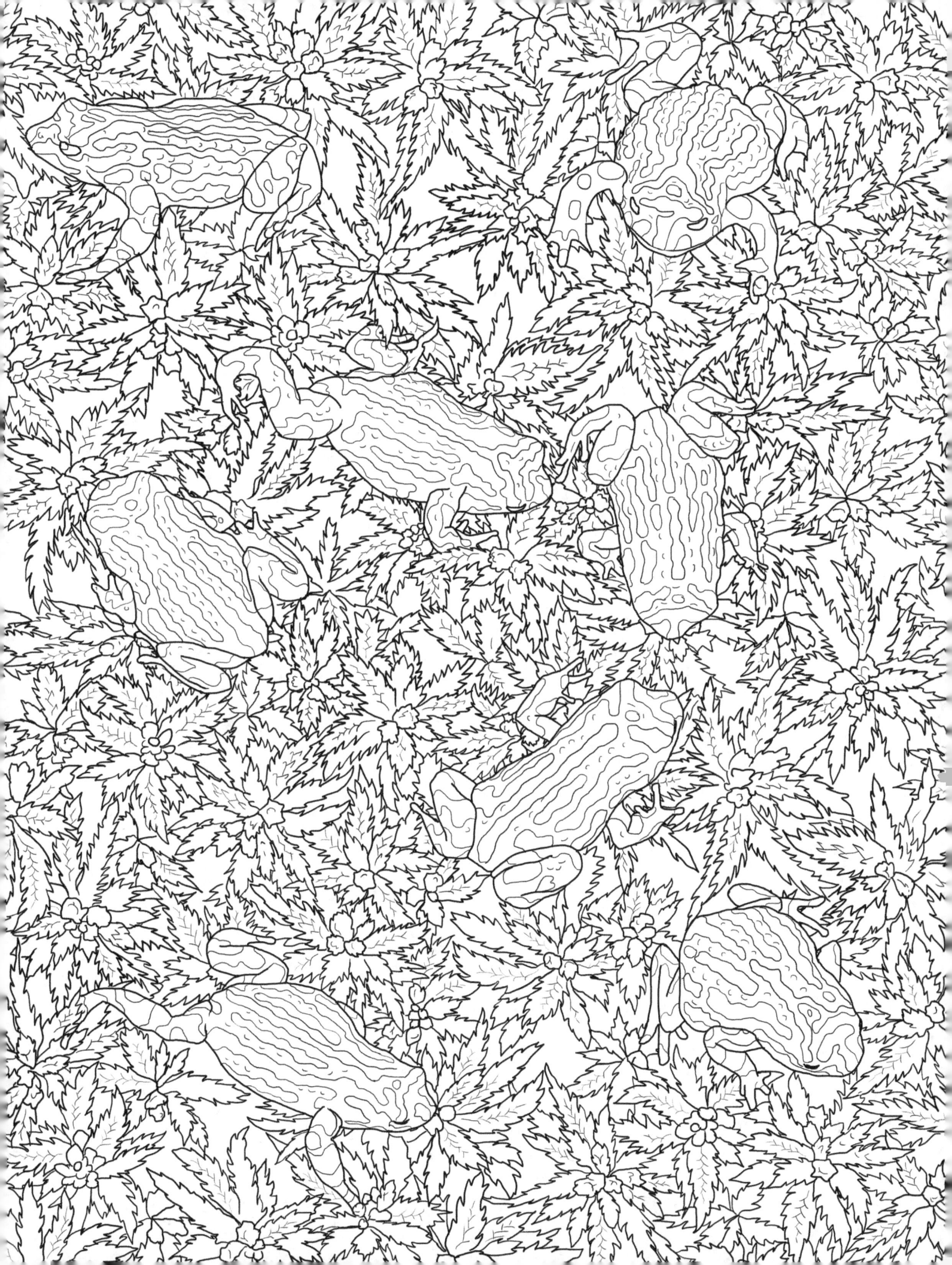

southern corroboree frog | *Pseudophryne corroboree*

southern corroboree frog | *Pseudophryne corroboree*

splendid wren | *Malurus splendens*

splendid wren | *Malurus splendens*

spotted parrotfish | *Cetoscarus ocellatus*

spotted parrotfish | *Cetoscarus ocellatus*

wedge-tailed eagle | *Aquila audax*

wedge-tailed eagle | *Aquila audax*

western pygmy possum | *Cercartetus concinnus*

woma python │ *Aspidites ramsayi*

woma python | *Aspidites ramsayi*

Boyd's forest dragon | *Hypsilurus boydii*

budgerigar | *Melopsittacus undulatus*

butterfly gurnard | *Lepidotrigla vanessa*

Cairns birdwing butterfly | *Ornithoptera euphorion*

fiddler beetle | *Eupoecila australasiae*

frilled-neck lizard | *Chlamydosaurus kingii*

greater blue-ringed octopus | *Hapalochlaena lunulata*

leafy seadragon | *Phycodurus eques*

Leichhardt's grasshopper | *Petasida ephippigera*

numbat | *Myrmecobius fasciatus*

Peacock spider | *Maratus volans*

quokka | *Setonix brachyurus*

rainbow lorikeet | *Trichoglossus moluccanus*

short-beaked echidna | *Tachyglossus aculeatus*

southern corroboree frog | *Pseudophryne corroboree*

splendid wren | *Malurus splendens*

spotted parrotfish | *Cetoscarus ocellatus*

wedge-tailed eagle | *Aquila audax*

western pygmy possum | *Cercartetus concinnus*

woma python | *Aspidites ramsayi*